YOU ARE HEALED

KENNETH COPELAND

KENNETH COPELAND
PUBLICATIONS

Unless otherwise noted, all scripture is from the *King James Version* of the Bible.

You Are Healed

ISBN-10 0-88114-733-8   30-0013
ISBN-13 978-0-88114-733-9

26 25 24 23 22 21   29 28 27 26 25 24

Kenneth Copeland Publications
Fort Worth, TX 76192-0001

For more information about Kenneth Copeland Ministries, visit kcm.org or call 1-800-600-7395 (U.S. only) or +1-817-852-6000.

Is Healing God's Will?

To know God's will about healing, you must first know what His Word says because His Word is His will. John 1:1, 14 says, "In the beginning was the Word, and the Word was with God, and the Word was God.... And the Word was made flesh, and dwelt among us, (and we beheld his glory, the glory as of the only begotten of the Father,) full of grace and truth."

Jesus of Nazareth was the Word of God made flesh—the total expression of God's will manifest in human form. This is what He said about Himself:

My meat is to do the will of him that sent me, and to finish his work (John 4:34).

He that believeth on me, believeth not on me, but on him that sent me. And he that seeth me seeth him that sent me (John 12:44-45).

I am the way, the truth, and the life: no man cometh unto the Father, but by me. If ye had known me, ye should have known my Father also…he that hath seen me hath seen the Father (see John 14:6-9).

If you want to see God, look at Jesus.

If you want to hear God, listen to Jesus.

If you want to know God's will, study the ministry of Jesus.

According to Hebrews 1:1-3, Jesus is God's Son—the heir of all things, the brightness of God's glory, the express image of God's person. *Jesus is the very image of Almighty God!* Everything He did, every move He made, every word He spoke was an extension of His Father in heaven.

There is no question Jesus came to do the will of the Father. In John 10:10 He said, "I am come that they might have life, and that they might have it more abundantly." Abundant life is God's will for the believer. Jesus explained very clearly how He would bring that abundant life into manifestation:

> And he came to Nazareth, where he had been brought up: and, as his custom was, he went into the

synagogue on the sabbath day, and stood up for to read. And there was delivered unto him the book of the prophet Esaias. And when he had opened the book, he found the place where it was written, The Spirit of the Lord is upon me, because he hath anointed me to preach the gospel to the poor; he hath sent me to heal the brokenhearted, to preach deliverance to the captives, and recovering of sight to the blind, to set at liberty them that are bruised, to preach the acceptable year of the Lord (Luke 4:16-19).

When He had finished reading, Jesus closed the book, sat down and said, "This day is this scripture fulfilled in your ears" (verse 21).

Jesus did what He said He would do: He preached the gospel, healed the sick, brought sight to the blind and delivered the captives. He taught in the synagogues of Galilee and the people were amazed. "And they were astonished at his doctrine: for his word was with power" (Luke 4:32). Every word going forth from His mouth brought deliverance and healing.

Jesus never turned away from healing anyone who came to Him in faith. He never said, "I can't heal you. God wants you to stay sick a little longer." He always responded to the faith of the people.

Acts 10:38 says: "How God anointed Jesus of Nazareth with the Holy Ghost and with power: who went about doing good, and healing *all* that were oppressed of the devil; for God was with him."

God wants His people healed and whole. He demonstrated this through Jesus. You can see His will toward healing expressed very simply in Luke 5:12-13: "And it came to pass, when he was in a certain city, behold a man full of leprosy: who seeing Jesus fell on his face, and besought him, saying, Lord, if thou wilt, thou canst make me clean. And he put forth his hand, and touched him, saying, I will: be thou clean. And immediately the leprosy departed from him."

When the leper asked, "Will you make me clean?" Jesus answered immediately, "I will: be thou clean."

The leper knew Jesus *could* heal him. The only question in his mind was whether or not Jesus *would*. This is the key point in receiving healing— the determining factor in acting by faith or unbelief. You know God can heal. The problem comes in knowing for certain that God *will* heal and that He will heal *you!* Until you realize in your own heart that God wants to heal you, you will never receive from Him. You can watch other people receive healing and still never receive it yourself.

To realize the truth of God's will for healing, you need to understand the full extent of your redemption. Healing is just as much a part of the plan of redemption as salvation, the Holy Spirit and heaven as your eternal home. To stay sick when Jesus has provided healing would be living far below your privileges as a child of God.

Let's view the plan of redemption through the eyes of Isaiah the prophet. He describes what was to happen at Calvary—the sacrifice, the pain, the suffering, the death. He gave a very accurate picture of Calvary, by the Holy Spirit, showing exactly what would happen in both the physical and the spiritual world: "Surely he hath borne our griefs, and carried our sorrows…" (Isaiah 53:4).

Note the first word of this verse: *Surely*—not maybe, not perhaps. It's a fact. *Surely* Jesus has borne our griefs and carried our sorrows! The *King James Version* gives an inaccurate translation of the original Hebrew words. The literal Hebrew translation of the words for *griefs* and *sorrows* should read, "Surely he hath borne our sickness, and carried our disease."

> But he was wounded for our transgressions, he was bruised for our iniquities: the chastisement of our peace was upon him; and with his stripes we

are healed. All we like sheep have gone astray; we have turned every one to his own way; and the Lord hath laid on him the iniquity of us all. He was oppressed, and he was afflicted, yet he opened not his mouth: he is brought as a lamb to the slaughter, and as a sheep before her shearers is dumb, so he openeth not his mouth. He was taken from prison and from judgment: and who shall declare his generation? for he was cut off out of the land of the living: for the transgression of my people was he stricken. And he made his grave with the wicked, and with the rich is his death; because he had done no violence, neither was any deceit in his mouth. Yet it pleased the

Lord to bruise him; he hath put him to grief… (Isaiah 53:5-10).

Most modern translations read, "It was God's will that He be bruised." It was the definite will and design of God that Jesus take all sickness and disease on Himself for us. His purpose was to free mankind from it.

Isaiah 53:11, The *Amplified Bible, Classic Edition* says: "He [God] shall see [the fruit] of the travail of His [Jesus'] soul and be satisfied." God would see the fruit of *Jesus'* travail and be satisfied! It does not satisfy God to see sickness and disease on believers today. He was satisfied when that sickness and disease was laid on Jesus. Many people think God wants them to stay sick, so He can get glory out of their travail, but that kind of thinking is a lie straight from the pit of hell!

To put sickness on you after it was put on Jesus would be a miscarriage of justice! You are not the sacrificial Lamb of Calvary. That sacrifice has already been made—it does not need to be made again. You need to receive His sacrifice made for you and appropriate its benefits into your life.

What was the fruit of Jesus' travail? Salvation, healing, love, joy, peace—the kingdom of God being born in the hearts of men. Praise God!

From these scriptures alone, you can know beyond doubt that God's will is for every person in Christ Jesus to be healed and made well. He paid the price, so we could receive it.

Any time a believer has a problem receiving healing, he usually suffers from ignorance of God's Word, ignorance of his rights and privileges in Jesus Christ. To fully understand your position, you need to realize what took place many centuries ago between God and a man named Abram. God approached Abram with a proposition. The agreement, or *covenant,* they made together is the basis of the entire New Testament. It was in behalf of this covenant that Jesus came to earth.

God's Covenant of Healing

Healing is not a new provision brought into being with the ministry of Jesus. Healing was provided for under the Abrahamic covenant. This is how that covenant came into existence:

And when Abram was ninety years old and nine, the Lord

appeared to Abram, and said unto him, I am the Almighty God; walk before me, and be thou perfect. And I will make my covenant between me and thee, and will multiply thee exceedingly. And Abram fell on his face: and God talked with him, saying, As for me, behold, my covenant is with thee, and thou shalt be a father of many nations. Neither shall thy name any more be called Abram, but thy name shall be Abraham; for a father of many nations have I made thee… And I will establish my covenant between me and thee and thy seed after thee in their generations for an everlasting covenant, to be a God unto thee, and to thy seed after thee (Genesis 17:1-5, 7).

When God appeared to Abram He said, "I am the Almighty God." The original Hebrew says, "I am El Shaddai." *El* means "supreme." *Shaddai* means "the Breasty One." He said, "I will be a God to you." In other words, "I will be all you need—your father, your mother, your nurse, your provider."

Realize the full significance of what took place between God and Abraham. They entered into a contract together. They made covenant together—an everlasting covenant, an absolute agreement. God said, "As for me, behold, my covenant is with thee." Then He sealed His side of the agreement by swearing an oath. In Genesis 22:16 God said, "By myself have I sworn." There was no higher power to swear by, so He swore by Himself. He gave His own word that He would bless Abraham and his seed. "That in blessing I will bless thee, and in multiplying I will multiply thy seed.... And in thy seed shall all the nations of the earth be blessed" (Genesis 22:17-18).

The Hebrew word *covenant* means "to cut," implying "where blood flows." A blood covenant is the strongest form of agreement on earth. Two parties agree to certain terms and then seal their agreement by the shedding of blood. The covenant made between God and Abraham was sealed through the act of circumcision. "This is my covenant, which ye shall keep, between me and you and thy seed after thee; Every man child among you shall be circumcised. And ye shall circumcise the flesh of your foreskin; and it shall be a token of the covenant betwixt me and you" (Genesis 17:10-11).

The shedding of blood was the

most vital act of the Old Testament. The blood shed in circumcision stood as a sign of agreement, a token of the covenant between God and man. El Shaddai agreed to bless Abraham and his descendants exceedingly. In return, He required them to live uprightly before Him.

But man continually sinned against God, failing to hold to the terms of the agreement. Again, the shedding of blood held the answer. The Levitical priesthood was instituted to offer blood sacrifices that would atone (or cover) for sin. Without the shedding of blood, there is no remission of sin (Hebrews 9:22). The offering of an innocent lamb on the altar covered the sin of God's covenant people for one year. God accepted these sacrifices in order to keep the Abrahamic covenant in force. This was the only way to bridge the gap between sin and righteousness.

Centuries later, the supreme blood sacrifice was made. Jesus of Nazareth came into the world, born of a virgin. When John the Baptist first saw Jesus he said, "Behold the Lamb of God, which taketh away the sin of the world" (John 1:29). Jesus was the sacrificial lamb offered upon the altar of the cross. He was the final sacrifice under the Abrahamic covenant. The blood He shed on the cross washed away forever the spot of sin. The Old Testament sacrifices only covered sin, but the New Testament sacrifice—Jesus, the spotless Son of God—completely did away with it. Hebrews 9:12 says, "Neither by the blood of goats and calves, but by his own blood he entered in once into the holy place, having obtained eternal redemption for us." By accepting His sacrifice, you stand before God clean and pure—just as if you had never sinned.

When sin entered the world, it brought with it the forces of destruction: death, sickness, poverty and fear. Jesus bore sin's penalty and, at the same time, did away with all the effects of it. Jesus paid the full price at Calvary, covering every area of human life: spiritual, mental, physical, financial and social. Our redemption is complete.

Galatians 3:13-14 says, "Christ hath redeemed us from the curse of the law, being made a curse for us: for it is written, Cursed is every one that hangeth on a tree: That the blessing of Abraham might come on the Gentiles through Jesus Christ; that we might receive the promise of the Spirit through faith."

"The curse of the Law" described in Deuteronomy 28:15 was the penalty for any person who disobeyed the statutes of the Levitical Law. It included every possible curse that could come on mankind: sickness, disease, poverty, lack, pain, suffering, etc. Verse 61 includes, "Also every sickness, and every plague, which is not written in the book of this law...."

Though Jesus lived a sinless life, He gave Himself to bear that curse as if He were the One who had sinned and disobeyed the Law. He took the punishment for all the sin of mankind. He bore the curse which included every sickness and every plague known to man. He bore pain and suffering. Why? So that we could, instead, receive the blessing when we accept His sacrifice as our own. Because we are in Christ, we are now Abraham's seed and heirs to the blessing.

Galatians 3:29 says, "And if ye be Christ's, then are ye Abraham's seed, and heirs according to the promise."

Deuteronomy 28 sets out the stipulations of this blessing and curse:

> And it shall come to pass, if thou shalt hearken diligently unto the voice of the Lord thy God, to observe and to do all his commandments which I command thee this day, that the Lord thy God will set thee on high above all nations of the earth: And all these blessings shall come on thee, and overtake thee, if thou shalt hearken unto the voice of the Lord thy God (verses 1-2).

Then verses 3-14 list all the blessings of the Law, describing prosperity in every area of life.

Jesus showed how healing is a part of this blessing when He ministered deliverance to a woman in Luke 13: 11-13: "And, behold, there was a woman which had a spirit of infirmity eighteen years, and was bowed together, and could in no wise lift up herself. And when Jesus saw her, he called her to him, and said unto her, Woman, thou art loosed from thine infirmity. And he laid his hands on her: and immediately she was made straight, and glorified God."

Because Jesus healed this woman on the sabbath day, the ruler of the synagogue was indignant; but Jesus answered him saying: "Thou hypocrite, doth not each one of you on the sabbath loose his ox or his ass from the stall, and lead him away to watering? And ought not this woman, being a daughter of Abraham, whom Satan hath bound, lo, these eighteen years, be loosed from this bond on the sabbath day?" (verses 15-16).

The Abrahamic covenant had been in force for many years. God's people could have walked in health and well-being, but they had become too preoccupied with their religious traditions. The result was a standard of living far below that which God had intended for them.

This woman was a daughter of Abraham and, because of that, her covenant right was to be loosed from her infirmity. Satan had been able to keep her bound for eighteen years for only one reason: because she was ignorant of her covenant with God. Jesus came and ministered as a prophet under the Abrahamic covenant. He healed the people according to that covenant. He came to set the captives free, and this woman was one of those captives. All she needed was for someone to tell her what was rightfully hers as a daughter of Abraham.

I have good news for you: If that woman could be delivered and set free because she was Abraham's seed, so can you on those same grounds. Because you believe in Jesus Christ and have accepted His sacrifice as your own, you are Abraham's seed and heir to the promise (Galatians 3:13). Praise God, that promise includes physical healing!

Satan has no right to put any sickness, disease or infirmity on your body. You are a child of God, a joint heir with Jesus and a citizen in the kingdom of God. You have a covenant with Almighty God, and one of your covenant rights is the right to a healthy body.

"I Want My People Well"

Some time ago, God dealt with me on the subject of healing and how important it is for believers to live free from sickness and disease. His words to me then were so strong they echoed in my spirit for weeks. He said, "I want My people well!"

God wants every believer to be healed and whole: "Beloved, I wish above all things that thou mayest prosper and be in health, even as thy soul prospereth" (3 John 2).

After Jesus was raised from the dead, He appeared to His disciples and issued certain decrees that would affect the world forever. Healing was one of those decrees. In Mark 16:15-18, Jesus said:

> Go ye into all the world, and preach the gospel to every creature. He that believeth and is baptized shall be saved; but he that believeth not shall be damned. And these signs shall follow them that believe; In my name shall they cast out devils; they shall speak with new tongues; They shall take up serpents; and if they drink any deadly thing, it shall not hurt them; they shall lay hands on the sick, and they shall recover.

These words are vitally important to every believer today. Jesus commanded the Church to go forth in His Name, and part of this Great Commission is that believers lay hands on the sick. At that moment, Jesus set the Church against sickness and disease.

Healing is God's masterstroke of evidence that He is alive and doing well. It is physical proof of His existence and willingness to meet our needs on every spiritual level.

No two people are exactly the same spiritually. Each is at his individual level of spiritual growth. But generally, there are three categories of spiritual life:

1. The world—sinners or unbelievers, who do not know God.

2. The carnally minded Christian—spiritual babies, who do not have God's Word working

proficiently in their lives.

3. The mature Christian—spiritual adults, skillful in the Word of God.

God's Word is designed to minister to individual needs at each level of spiritual growth.

In 1 Corinthians 3:1-3, Paul refers to the two levels of spiritual maturity within the Body of Christ, the Church: "And I, brethren, could not speak unto you as unto spiritual, but as unto carnal, even as unto babes in Christ. I have fed you with milk, and not with meat: for hitherto ye were not able to bear it, neither yet now are ye able. For ye are yet carnal: for whereas there is among you envying, and strife, and divisions, are ye not carnal, and walk as men?"

Paul could not teach the Corinthian believers about deeper spiritual things because they were not mature enough to understand. They were "babes in Christ," and he had to feed them with "milk"—basic principles of faith—as you would feed a tiny baby. Hebrews 5:13 says, "For every one that useth milk is unskillful in the word of righteousness: for he is a babe." First Peter 2:2 says, "As newborn babes, desire the sincere milk of the word, that ye may grow thereby."

When you accepted Jesus as Savior and made Him the Lord of your life, you were "born of God" (1 John 5:1). According to 1 Peter 1:23, you were "born again," not of corruptible seed, but of incorruptible, by the Word of God. At that moment, you joined the family of God and entered into spiritual affairs as a newborn baby. If, since that time, you have never fed on the milk of the Word, you are still a spiritual baby. You will not yet be able to operate proficiently in faith without a knowledge of the Word.

A baby does not grow to adulthood overnight, so a new believer should not expect to operate as a mature Christian after only a few days. It takes time spent in God's Word to grow and mature spiritually.

The first step to spiritual maturity is to realize your position in God. You are His child and a joint heir with Jesus. Romans 8:16-17 says: "The Spirit itself beareth witness with our spirit, that we are the children of God: and if children, then heirs; heirs of God, and joint-heirs with Christ; if so be that we suffer with him, that we may be also glorified together." You are entitled to all the rights and privileges in the kingdom of God, and one of these rights is health and healing.

You will never fully realize or understand healing until you know beyond any doubt that God's will is for you to be healed. As we have seen, God wants you healed! He wants you whole! He wants you to grow in the Word and walk in His perfect will just as Jesus did. Whether or not you accept this and purpose to walk in the reality of the truth, is your decision.

I urge you to accept it now and begin to see His will carried out in your life. Begin seeing yourself healed and whole. Put God's Word concerning healing in your heart, meditate and think about it, then speak it out boldly over yourself. His Word will not return to Him void, but it will accomplish what it was sent to do (Isaiah 55:11).

Prayer for Salvation and Baptism in the Holy Spirit

Heavenly Father, I come to You in the Name of Jesus. Your Word says, "Whosoever shall call on the name of the Lord shall be saved" (Acts 2:21). I am calling on You. I pray and ask Jesus to come into my heart and be Lord over my life according to Romans 10:9-10: "If thou shalt confess with thy mouth the Lord Jesus, and shalt believe in thine heart that God hath raised him from the dead, thou shalt be saved. For with the heart man believeth unto righteousness; and with the mouth confession is made unto salvation." I do that now. I confess that Jesus is Lord, and I believe in my heart that God raised Him from the dead. I repent of sin. I renounce it. I renounce the devil and everything he stands for. Jesus is my Lord.

I am now reborn! I am a Christian—a child of Almighty God! I am saved! You also said in Your Word, "If ye then, being evil, know how to give good gifts unto your children: HOW MUCH MORE shall your heavenly Father give the Holy Spirit to them that ask him?" (Luke 11:13). I'm also asking You to fill me with the Holy Spirit. Holy Spirit, rise up within me as I praise God. I fully expect to speak with other tongues as You give me the utterance (Acts 2:4). In Jesus' Name. Amen!

Begin to praise God for filling you with the Holy Spirit. Speak those words and syllables you receive—not in your own language, but the language given to you by the Holy Spirit. You have to use your own voice. God will not force you to speak. Don't be concerned with how it sounds. It is a heavenly language!

Continue with the blessing God has given you and pray in the spirit every day.

You are a born-again, Spirit-filled believer. You'll never be the same!

Find a good church that boldly preaches God's Word and obeys it. Become part of a church family who will love and care for you as you love and care for them.

We need to be connected to each other. It increases our strength in God. It's God's plan for us.

Make it a habit to watch the *Believer's Voice of Victory* broadcast and VICTORY Channel® and become a doer of the Word, who is blessed in his doing (James 1:22-25).

About the Author

Kenneth Copeland is co-founder and president of Kenneth Copeland Ministries in Fort Worth, Texas, and best-selling author of books that include *Honor—Walking in Honesty, Truth and Integrity,* and *THE BLESSING of The LORD Makes Rich and He Adds No Sorrow With It.*

Since 1967, Kenneth has been a minister of the gospel of Christ and teacher of God's WORD. He is also the artist on award-winning albums such as his Grammy-nominated *Only the Redeemed, In His Presence, He Is Jehovah, Just a Closer Walk* and *Big Band Gospel.* He also co-stars as the character Wichita Slim in the children's adventure videos *The Gunslinger, Covenant Rider* and the movie *The Treasure of Eagle Mountain,* and as Daniel Lyon in the Commander Kellie and the Superkids™ videos *Armor of Light* and *Judgment: The Trial of Commander Kellie.* Kenneth also co-stars as a Hispanic godfather in the 2009 and 2016 movies *The Rally and The Rally 2: Breaking the Curse.*

With the help of offices and staff in the United States, Canada, England, Australia, South Africa, Ukraine and Latin America, Kenneth is fulfilling his vision to boldly preach the uncompromised WORD of God from the top of the world, to the bottom, and all the way around the middle. His ministry reaches millions of people worldwide through daily and Sunday TV broadcasts, magazines, teaching audios and videos, conventions and campaigns, and the World Wide Web.

Learn more about Kenneth Copeland Ministries by visiting our website at **kcm.org.**

When the Lord first spoke to Kenneth and Gloria Copeland about starting the *Believer's Voice of Victory* magazine...

He said: *This is your seed. Give it to everyone who ever responds to your ministry, and don't ever allow anyone to pay for a subscription!*

For more than 50 years, it has been the joy of Kenneth Copeland Ministries to bring the good news to believers. Readers enjoy teaching from ministers who write from lives of living contact with God, and testimonies from believers experiencing victory through God's Word in their everyday lives.

Today, the *BVOV* magazine is mailed monthly, bringing encouragement and blessing to believers around the world. Many even use it as a ministry tool, passing it on to others who desire to know Jesus and grow in their faith!

Request your FREE subscription to the
***Believer's Voice of Victory* magazine today!**

Go to **freevictory.com** to subscribe online, or call us at **1-800-600-7395** (U.S. only) or **+1-817-852-6000**.

We're Here for You!

Your growth in God's Word and your victory in Jesus are at the very center of our hearts. In every way God has equipped us, we will help you deal with the issues facing you, so you can be the **victorious overcomer** He has planned for you to be.

The mission of Kenneth Copeland Ministries is about all of us growing and going together. Our prayer is that you will take full advantage of all The LORD has given us to share with you.

Wherever you are in the world, you can watch the *Believer's Voice of Victory* broadcast on television (check local listings), kcm.org and digital streaming devices like Roku®. You can also watch the broadcast as well as programs from dozens of ministers you can trust on our 24/7 faith network—Victory Channel®. Visit govictory.com for show listings and all the ways to watch.

Our website, **kcm.org,** gives you access to every resource we've developed for your victory. And, you can find contact information for our international offices in Africa, Australia, Canada, Europe, Latin America, Ukraine and our headquarters in the United States.

Each office is staffed with devoted men and women, ready to serve and pray with you. You can contact the worldwide office nearest you for assistance, and you can call us for prayer at our U.S. number, +1-817-852-6000, seven days a week!

We encourage you to connect with us often and let us be part of your everyday walk of faith!

Jesus Is LORD!

Kenneth & Gloria Copeland

Kenneth and Gloria Copeland